SCRAPPED PRINCESS
SCRAPPED PRINCESS

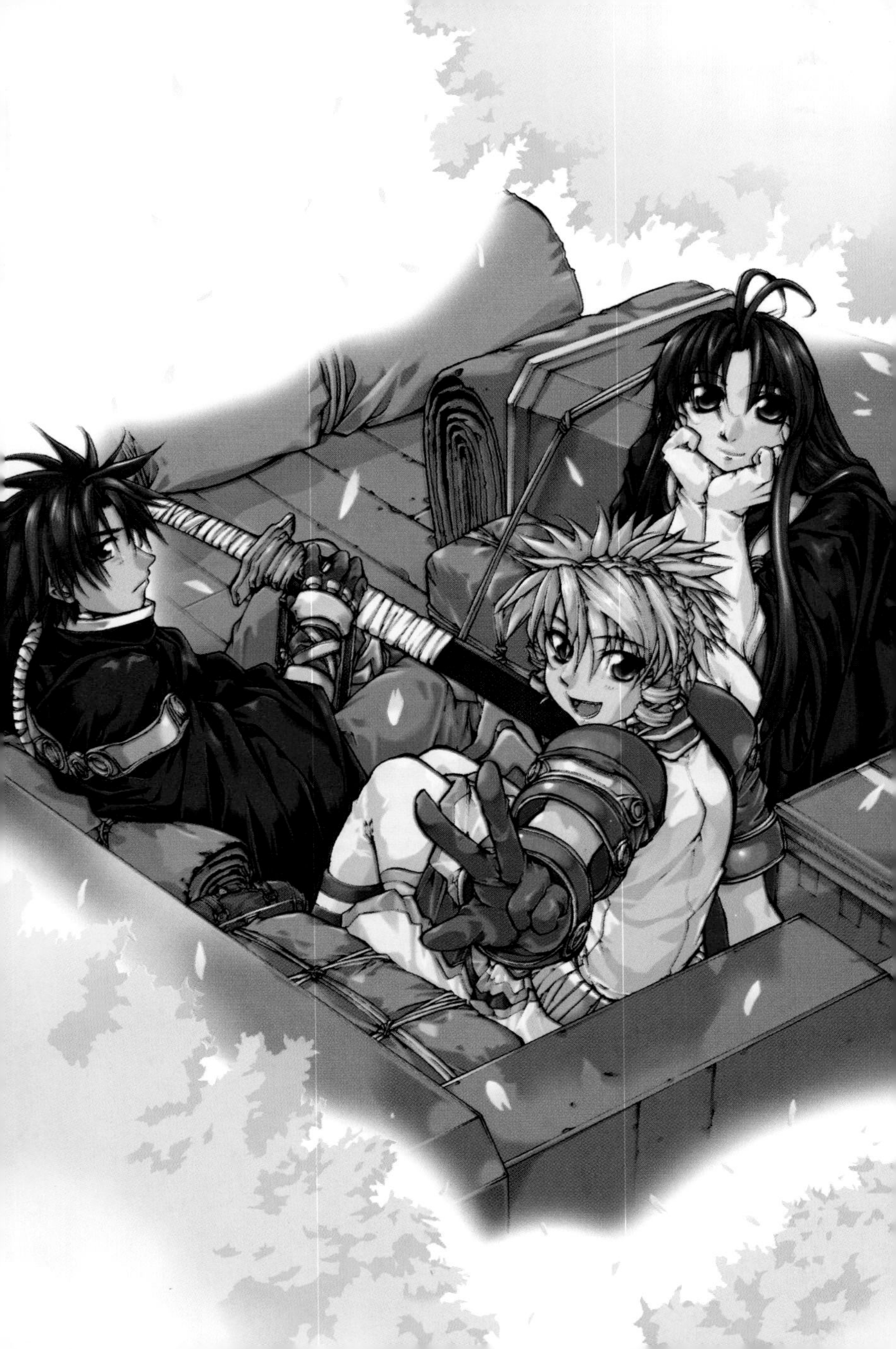

Original work: Ichiro Sakaki

Original Character Design: Yukinobu Azumi

Illustrations: Go Yabuki

HAMBURG // LONDON // LOS ANGELES // TOKYO

Scrapped Princess Vol. 2

Story: Ichiro Sakaki
Art: Go Yabuki
Character Plan: Yukinobu Azumi

Translation - Alethea Nibley
English Adaptation - Liesl M. Bradner
Retouch and Lettering - Chris Anderson
Production Artist - James Dashiell
Cover Design - Al-Insan Lashley

Editor - Julie Taylor
Digital Imaging Manager - Chris Buford
Production Managers - Jennifer Miller and Mutsumi Miyazaki
Managing Editor - Lindsey Johnston
VP of Production - Ron Klamert
Publisher and E.I.C. - Mike Kiley
President and C.O.O. - John Parker
C.E.O. - Stuart Levy

A  Manga

TOKYOPOP Inc.
5900 Wilshire Blvd. Suite 2000
Los Angeles, CA 90036

E-mail: info@TOKYOPOP.com
Come visit us online at www.TOKYOPOP.com

ISBN: 1-59532-982-X

First TOKYOPOP printing: January 2006

10 9 8 7 6 5 4 3 2 1

Printed in Canada

Previously In

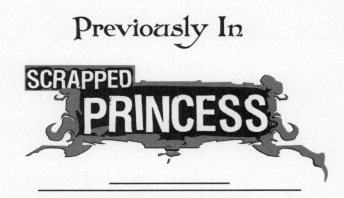

Fifteen years ago, a set of twins—a girl and a boy—was born to the king of Linevan. Shortly after their birth, a prophecy foretold that when the girl turned 16, she would bring about the end of humanity. To avoid this terrible fate, the king ordered the princess disposed of—scrapped! She miraculously survived and was raised away from the kingdom that would kill her. But now she has turned 15, the king's guards have caught wind that she's still alive...and they set out to finish the job!

Chapter Seven: Unfulfilled Feelings Part One
PACIFICA, IN FRONT OF YOU!!
AH!!!
HA HA HA!
OW OW OW...
ARE YOU OKAY?

I'M SO SORRY!!!
HERE. IS THIS YOURS?
THANK YOU.
THIS IS... VERY IMPORTANT TO ME.
AHH. I'M GLAD I FOUND IT.
IS SHE THERE?!
WELL, I'M IN A HURRY, SO...
Ah! You forgot this!
......?

UGH!
UGH!
SHE'S OVER HERE!! GO AROUND AND CATCH HER!!
I HAVE TO GET AWAY. I DON'T WANT TO GO BACK THERE EVER AGAIN!!
UGH!
UGH!

A DEAD END.
WHAT SHOULD I DO?
THERE SHE IS! OVER HERE!!
ビクッ

AAAHHH!!
?!
AH ...
UGH ...
MY BODY... WON'T MOVE.
I WONDER IF I'LL DIE LIKE THIS.
BEFORE THAT HAPPENS, I WANT TO...

UGH ...
...SEE HIM ONE MORE TIME.
UGH ...

HEY!
STOP!
WE'RE LOOKING FOR A RUNAWAY HARLOT. HAVE YOU SEEN HER?
SHE HAD A BUTTERFLY TATTOO ON HER SHOULDER, SO I THINK YOU'D RECOGNIZE HER.
TATTOO?
HEY, APPARENTLY SHE'S THAT WAY. LET'S GO!
SHANNON-NII! THE HARLOT THEY WERE TALKING ABOUT...
YEAH, SHE'S PROBABLY --

WHAT WILL HAPPEN TO HER IF SHE'S CAUGHT?
HARLOTS ARE GENERALLY GIRLS WHO HAVE BEEN SOLD. THERE'S NO TELLING WHAT WILL HAPPEN TO HER IF THEY CATCH HER.
THEN WE HAVE TO HELP HER!!
IT'S NOT LIKE SHE WANTED TO BE A HARLOT! THAT'S JUST TERRIBLE!!
BUT WE'RE FUGITIVES TOO. WE SHOULDN'T GET INVOLVED. IT'S TOO RECKLESS.
BUT...
WE HAVE TO GIVE THIS BACK TO HER. SHE SAID IT WAS IMPORTANT.
YOU'RE RIGHT. WE SHOULD MAKE SURE SHE GETS IT BACK.

PEOPLE HAVE BEEN TRYING TO KILL HER SINCE THE DAY SHE WAS BORN.
NONE OF THE PEOPLE AROUND HER WILL HELP. THEY JUST LOOK THE OTHER WAY.
ALL BECAUSE SHE HAS BEEN DESIGNATED AS THE BEING WHO WILL DESTROY THIS WORLD... THE SCRAPPED PRINCESS.
THAT'S WHY SHE CAN'T LEAVE LUTEA ALONE.

GIVIN US A HARD TIME!
YOU CAN'T GET AWAY NOW.
...
LUTEA! COME HERE!!
NOW THEN...
AHHH. DON'T BE TOO ROUGH WITH HER.
WHAT DO I DO?
....
GANGING UP ON ONE WOMAN-- THAT'S NOT VERY POLITE!

NOW I'D LIKE YOU TO LET THE GIRL GO.

SHE'S A HARLOT, YOU KNOW? YOU DON'T NEED TO GO THROUGH SO MUCH TROUBLE.

OR...OR WHAT? YOU LIKE HER?

......

F-FINE. WE'LL LET HER GO. IN EXCHANGE, LET HIM GO AT THE SAME TIME!
SOUNDS GOOD.

ドッ

FOOL!

GET HIM!!

UGH.
EEK!
ビク

RE--
REMEMBER THIS!!
I'M SO GLAD YOU'RE SAFE! THIS IS FOR YOU!
UH...HUH? WHAT'S WRONG?
....
THIS...IS IMPORTANT TO YOU, ISN'T IT?

SHE'S BEEN LIKE THIS FOR A WHILE. SHE MUST BE IN TREMENDOUS SHOCK.
CAN'T YOU DO SOMETHING, RAQUEL?
WE CAN'T JUST LEAVE HER LIKE THIS. AND I HAVE NO IDEA WHERE WE SHOULD TAKE HER.

THE FOREST.

H-HEY, WHERE ARE YOU GOING?!

SHANNON-NII! RAQUEL-NEE, LISTEN!! SHE'S SAYING SOMETHING!

WHERE ON EARTH IS SHE TRYING TO GO?

I DON'T KNOW BUT SHE WAS SAYING SOMETHING ABOUT "THE FOREST."

I ACTUALLY STARTED ASGARD UP A WHILE AGO, BUT I CAN'T PICK UP A RESPONSE TO HER.
COULD SHE BE...?
HEY, YOU WERE SAYING SOMETHING ABOUT THE FOREST, BUT WHAT'S THERE?!
COME ON! YOU MIGHT GET CAUGHT BY ANOTHER GROUP OF WEIRDOES.
IT'S SAFER TO GO WITH US THAN BY YOURSELF.
AAAAHHH... ARE YOU LISTENING?

RAQUEL-NEE, WHAT SHOULD WE DO?
......
......
チラ
THERE, THERE.
I'M INTERESTED IN WHO SHE IS. LET'S SEE WHAT SHE DOES.

WHAT'S GOING ON?! SHANNON-NII!

Chapter Eight: Unfulfilled Feelings Part Two
WHAT'S GOING ON, SHANNON-NII?

Chapter Eight: Unfulfilled Feelings
Part Two

WERE YOU THE ONE I CRASHED INTO IN TOWN?!

IF WE DON'T CLEAR THAT UP, I DON'T KNOW WHICH OF YOU TO GIVE THIS BACK TO.

......
SHE SAID THIS WAS VERY IMPORTANT TO HER.
WHEN I FOUND OUT YOU WERE RUNNING AWAY AND THIS WAS ALL YOU HAD... I THOUGHT IT WAS REALLY IMPORTANT THAT I GET IT BACK TO YOU, NO MATTER WHAT.
BECAUSE I KNOW WHAT THAT'S LIKE...
PENDANT ...
スッ
UNFUL-FILLED FEELINGS ...

I HAVE TO GIVE IT TO HIM.
YOU DO RECOGNIZE IT...THIS PENDANT?!
PACIFICA?
MAY I TALK TO YOU?
I HAVEN'T TOLD YOU THIS, BUT I COULDN'T PICK UP A RESPONSE TO HER WITH ASGARD.
EH?
WHAT DO YOU MEAN?

HER RESPONSE ...
...IS THE SAME AS BEFORE WHEN WE MET XI WANG MU.
IN OTHER WORDS ...
...THAT GIRL ISN'T HUMAN.
YOU MEAN SOMETHING CHANGED *INTO* HER?

SHOW US
YOUR TRUE
FORM!!

JUST A--!
SHANNON-NII!!

THAT'S A...
...MUD MAN?!
THAT IS?

WHAT'S A MUD MAN?

HMM...

I DON'T KNOW MUCH ABOUT THEM.

THEY TAKE LOST CHILDREN TO THEIR MOTHERS OR SOMETHING LIKE THAT.

HMMM.

HMM.
WHY DID YOU NEED TO TURN INTO LUTEA?
....
NO GOOD, HUH?
I HAVE TO...
...GO SEE HIM.
IN TOWN... THE PENDANT.

......
SHANNON-NII.
WHAT?
IT SEEMS LIKE THERE IS SOMEWHERE SHE WANTS TO GO.
?
SHE COULDN'T CONVEY HER FEELINGS, SO I'M GOING TO GRANT HER LAST WISH.

SHANNON-NII, LET'S TAKE HER THERE!

......

I DON'T THINK THAT'S SUCH A GOOD IDEA.
WHY?!

WE WEREN'T THE ONES WHO TOOK ON THE TASK OF DELIVERING HER FEELINGS. THE MUD MAN DID THAT.

WE'RE FUGITIVES. WE SHOULDN'T GET INVOLVED. IT'S TOO RISKY.
WE CAN'T DO THAT!!
WE'RE ALREADY INVOLVED!!
WE CAN'T COME THIS FAR AND THEN ACT LIKE WE DON'T CARE!

LISTEN TO ME.
THE ACTUAL PERSON IS ALREADY DEAD. WHAT WOULD COME OF US TELLING THE MUD MAN?
THAT'S EXACTLY WHY.
IT'S BECAUSE SHE'S GONE THAT WE HAVE TO TELL HIM!!

...IS SO SAD.
FOR NO ONE TO HAVE KNOWN THAT SHE WAS ALIVE OR THAT SHE DIED...

THAT SOUNDS A LITTLE HYPOCRITICAL.

IT MIGHT BE, BUT...

BY CONVEYING THE FEELINGS OF THE DEAD...

...YOU LEAVE PROOF THAT THEY LIVED? IS THAT WHAT YOU'RE SAYING?

HEH.
OKAY.
THANKS, SHANNON-NII!
WAH!

I WANT TO SEE HIM ONE MORE TIME.
AND TELL HIM...

BECAUSE IT WAS DECIDED THAT I WOULD BE SOLD.
AT THE TIME... I LIED.
BUT WHAT I REALLY FELT...

ALONG WITH THAT PENDANT... I WANT TO CONVEY MY FEELINGS TO HIM.
チュン
WE'VE GOT A PRETTY GOOD IDEA OF WHERE THIS PLACE IS FROM WHAT THE MUD MAN TOLD US.
SO, YOU READY TO GO?!

YEAH!
......
THANK...YOU...
VERY...MUCH
....
NO
PROBLEM.
LET'S
GO!

WAAAHH!
Chapter Nine: Lutea's Wish
WHAT HAPPENED? THAT GROUP PROTECTING LUTEA IS UNUSUALLY STRONG.
AH...
COULD IT BE?
THAT THEY'RE THE GROUP WITH THE BOUNTY ON THEIR HEADS? THE SCRAPPED PRINCESS PARTY?

Chapter Nine: Lutea's Wish

I THINK WE LOST THEM.
GOOD. THEN WE DON'T HAVE TO FIGHT.
HEH HEH HEH! LOOKS LIKE IT'S OKAY NOW.
YOU'RE PRETTY POPULAR.
?
POP... ULAR?
Heh heh
WELL, YOU'RE NOTHING COMPARED TO ME!!
WHAT YOU ARE IS *INFAMOUS*.
WHAT WAS THAT?!!

WE CAN FINALLY SEE IT.
HEY! IS THIS THE TOWN?

YES, I
HINK SO.
ビッ
キョトン
IT LOOKS LIKE WE'LL BE ABLE TO GET HER THERE AFTER ALL.
SHANNON, THEY'RE HERE!

THAT'S STRANGE. IT SEEMS LIKE THERE ARE MORE OF THEM THAN BEFORE.

THEY MUST'VE FIGURED OUT WHO WE ARE.

RAQUEL, TAKE THE REINS.
?
IT SHOULD BE FINE IF WE CAN CATCH UP TO THEM SOON.
WHATEVER YOU DO, DON'T LET THEM GET AWAY!!
IF WE CATCH THEM, WE'LL GET A HUGE REWARD!

H-HEY!!
WHA--?!
YOU'RE
--!!

WHAT'S WRONG? AREN'T YOU GOING TO CATCH ME?

I THINK I CAN DRAW THEM AWAY.

YES.
THIS IS A PRETTY SMALL TOWN.
I WONDER IF HE'S OKAY?
SHANNON WI BE FINE.
MORE IMPORTANT, WE HAVE SOMETHING TO DO, DON'T WE?

THAT'S RIGHT!!
LET'S DO OUR BEST TO FIND HIM!!
YES.
AAHH... IT'S ALREADY NIGHTTIME.
IT'S A GOOD THING THERE WERE PEOPLE WHO KNEW LUTEA.
NOW WE KNOW WHERE WE NEED TO GO.

I THINK THIS IS THE PLACE.
LUTE DO YO RECOGN THIS PL
YES!
IT MATCHES HER MEMORIES.
MEMORIES?
YES!

HER LOVE FOR HIM... HER SADNESS AT NOT BEING ABLE TO SHARE THEIR LIFE TOGETHER...

WHAT ON EARTH DID SHE WANT? WHAT WERE THE FEELINGS SHE COULDN'T CONVEY?

TELLING HIM
LUTEA'S
FEELINGS
HERE...
...MIGHT
BECOME A
BURDEN TO
HIM.
LUTEA, THE GI
WHO DIED...
...WOULD SHE
REALLY WANT
THAT?

……?
キョトン
……
LET'S RETHINK ABOUT WHAT IT WOULD MEAN TO CONVEY HER FEELINGS.
LET'S THINK ABOUT OTHER PEOPLE'S FEELINGS...
FEELINGS ...

......
THANK YOU. THIS IS VERY IMPORTANT TO ME.
OH YEAH!
THE PENDANT SHE SAID WAS SO IMPORTANT-- I'M SURE IT'S PACKED WITH LOTS OF FEELINGS!
IF WE GIVE THAT TO HIM, IT WILL TELL HIM HER FEELINGS!!
YOU'RE
LET'S BRING THE PENDANT TO HIM.

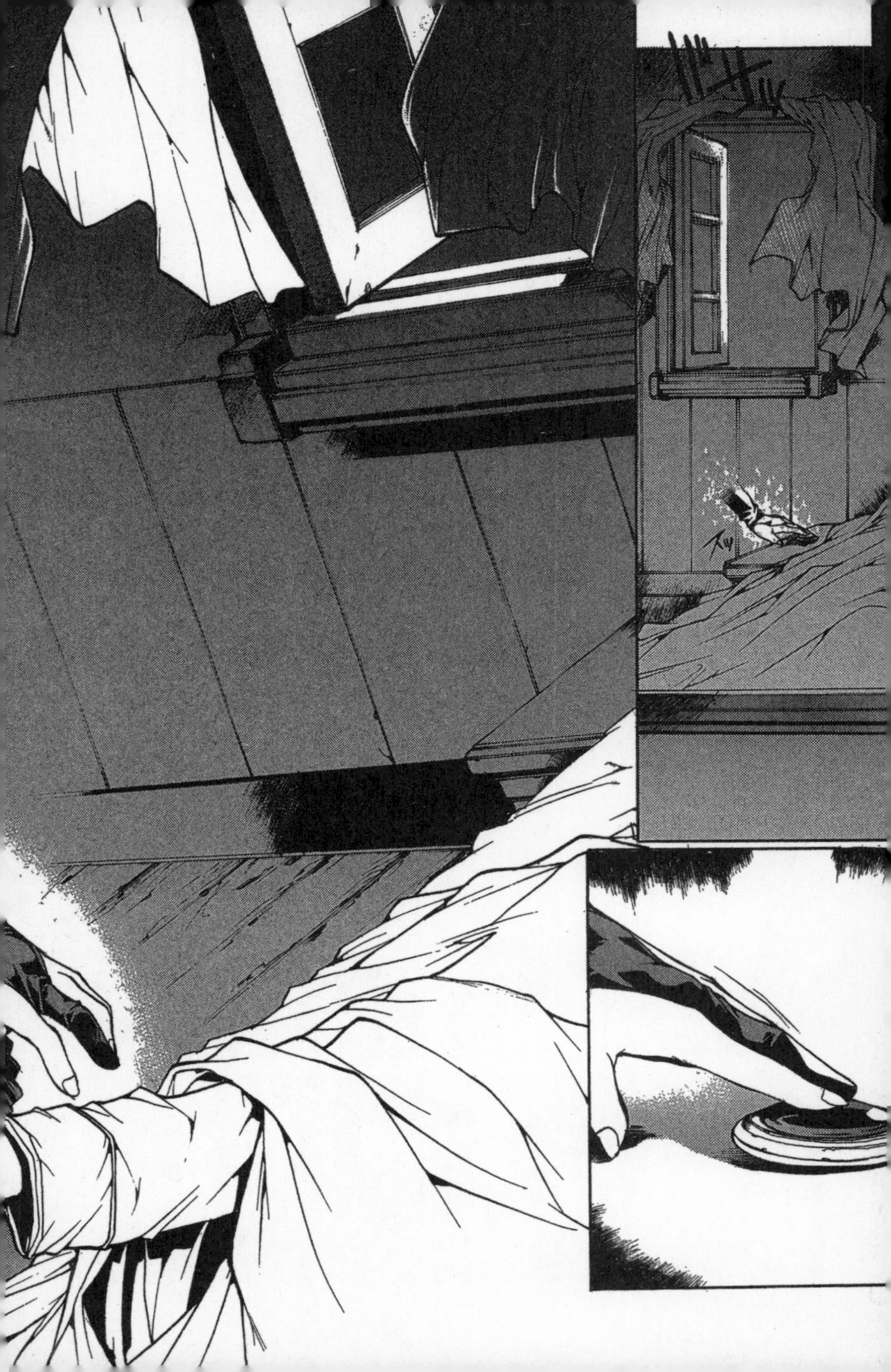

UHH.
I WONDER IF LUTEA IS OKAY?
OH, I MADE SURE TO CAST A SPELL ON HER. SHE'LL BE FINE!
Heh heh.
THAT'S WHAT MAKES ME NERVOUS.
IT LOOKS LIKE THINGS WENT WELL.
AH, SHANNON-NII!
HOW DID EVERYTHING GO?

I DON'T THINK THEY'LL BE COMING AFTER US ANYMORE.
IT LOOKS LIKE SHE'S BACK.
WELCOME BACK.
DID IT GO WELL?
コク
WELL THEN ...
LET'S GO!!

GOOD MORNING!
MM.
I HAD A DREAM LAST NIGHT.
IT FELT FAMILIAR, BUT PAINFULLY SAD TOO.

Chapter Ten: What She Wants

コク
RAQUEL, TAKE PACIFICA AND LUTEA AND CROSS THE RIVER.

Chapter Ten: What She Wants

IT HAD TO BE PURGERS, OF ALL THINGS.

HERE THEY COME!!

THIS IS CRAZY! I'M NOT GETTING ANYWHERE!
IS THERE SOME-THING I CAN USE?
THIS WATER?
THAT DRIFTWOOD DAM...IF I COULD BREAK IT.
?!
SHANNON!

TCH!
NO...
IF THEY THROW AT THE SAME TIME...
GET DOWN! PACIFICA!!

LUTEA !!
EH?!
KUH!
RAQUEL!! HIT THAT DRIFTWOOD!

HOLY BOW, DE-STROY!
EH?!

SHANNON-NII! HURRY!!
SHANNON!

SHANNON-NII!!
NEVER MIND ME.
WHAT ABOUT LUTEA'S WOUNDS?!
WELL... HER WOUNDS ARE ALREADY CLOSING UP.
I WONDER IF IT'S BECAUSE SHE'S A MUD MAN?
Th-the wounds are closing!
ANYWAY...
WE HAVE LUTEA TO THANK.
Over here, this way!
WHAT HAPPENED TO THE PURGERS, RAQUEL?
IT SEEMS THEY HAVE FLED OUTSIDE MY DETECTION.

ARE YOU HURT?
スッ

NO.
WHAT ABOUT YOU?
I'M ALL RIGHT.
I SEE.

ペコ
THANK YOU FOR PROTECTING PACIFICA. YOU HAVE MY GRATITUDE.

YEAH, THANK YOU, LUTEA.
......

RIGHT NOW, WE NEED TO FIND A PLACE WE CAN CATCH OUR BREATH.

IT'S A GOOD THING THAT THIS CABIN WAS HERE.
YES...
...LET'S STAY HERE UNTIL THE RAIN STOPS.
NOW WE CAN WARM UP.
MMM.

LUUUTEA! WHY ARE YOU STARING INTO SPACE?

I WAS THINKING.

I'VE HAD A STRANGE SENSATION SINCE THE TWO OF YOU THANKED ME EARLIER.

STRANGE SENSATION?

BUT THIS MYSTERIOUS SENSATION.
THAT HAS BEEN INSIDE ME SINCE EARLIER... WHAT COULD IT BE?
I HAVE A QUESTION. DO MUD MEN FEEL HUMAN EMOTIONS AND STUFF?
NO.
I GOT IT!
YOU'VE STARTED TO FEEL THEM!
?

I BET THAT'S THE FEELING CALLED "HAPPINESS."
THIS IS... WHAT THEY CALL HAPPINESS?
IT PROBABLY IS!
IF IT WAS ME, I WOULD BE HAPPY IF SOMEONE THANKED ME!

HEY, RAQUEL.

ABOUT LUTEA...

I THINK WE SHOULD LEAVE HER HERE. WHAT DO YOU THINK?

IF SHE STAYS WITH US, WE'D ONLY BE PUTTING HER IN DANGER.

AND IF WE LEFT HER WITH SOMEONE ELSE, HER UNPREDICTABLE ACTIONS COULD AUSE PROBLEMS.

I'LL TELL PACIFICA LATER.
I'VE ALREADY HEARD!
I'M TOTALLY AGAINST IT!! HOW CAN YOU MAKE A DECISION WITHOUT EVEN CONSULTING THE PERSON INVOLVED?!
WE SHOULD TREAT LUTEA MORE LIKE A PERSON. IF WE LEAVE HER HERE, IT'S THE SAME AS ABANDONING HER!!
WE KNOW THAT. WE DON'T MEAN TO TREAT HER LIKE A THING, BUT THE FACT IS LUTEA IS A MUD MAN.
FROM WHAT I'VE SEEN UP UNTIL NOW, I DON'T THINK THAT MUD MEN HAVE FEELINGS OR EMOTIONS.

THAT'S NOT TRUE! I FOUND OUT TALKING TO HER JUST NOW! SHE DOES HAVE FEELINGS!!
?!
WHEN WE THANKED LUTEA EARLIER, THAT MADE HER HAPPY.
SHE HAS EMOTIONS, JUST LIKE HUMANS!!
BESIDES, IF WE LEAVE HER HERE, SHE'LL BE ALL ALONE.
IF IT WAS ME, I WOULDN'T BE ABLE TO HANDLE BEING ALONE.

I UNDERSTAND WHAT YOU'RE SAYING, SHANNON-NII.
BUT THERE IS ANOTHER WAY, ISN'T THERE?
PACIFICA'S RIGHT.
IF WE LEAV
LUTEA HERE
WE'D BE JUST LIKE THE PEOPLE CHASING AFTER PACIFICA, THE SCRAPPED PRINCESS.
LUTEA, I'M SORRY. WHAT DO YOU WANT TO DO?

I...
...WANT TO BE OF SERVICE TO YOU ALL.
I SEE.
WELCOME TO THE GROUP.

SHANNON...
YEAH, IT'S BETTER THIS WAY.
PACIFICA-SAN.
?

I'M...
...HAPPY!
OH?!
LUTEA, YOU'RE SMILING!
...

RAQUEL ...
YES, THERE ARE FOUR RE-SPONSES.
THE PURGERS ARE HERE?

According to the oracle of St. Grendel ...

...ONE "PRINCES WAS BURIED DARKNES

BUT THAT "PRINCESS" WAS SECRETLY RESCUED.

SHE WAS GIVEN THE NAME PACIFICA.

AND FOR FOURTEEN YEARS WAS RAISED AS A GIRL.

PACIFICA IS THE ONE FORETOLD
TO BECOME THE POISON THAT
WOULD DESTROY THE WORLD,
THE SCRAPPED PRINCESS.

Chapter Eleven: Atonement Part One

EXCUSE ME...

COULD WE STAY HERE FOR THE NIGHT?

YOU HAVE EYES, DON'T YOU?

YOU'VE SEEN THE HOUSES IN THIS VILLAGE. THERE'S NOWHERE TO STAY.

BESIDES, I DON'T LIKE OUTSIDERS.

AHH...

ACHOO!
OH MY!
ずず
UGH ...
STOP IT!
OH...THIS BEAUTIFUL, DELICATE MAIDEN WILL HAVE TO SLEEP OUTSIDE IN THE COLD AGAIN.
BEAUTIFUL, DELICATE MAIDEN ASIDE, I'M PRETTY SICK OF STARING AT THE STARS.
HA HA HA...

HMM... WELL, ALL RIGHT.
IF YOU WANT TO STAY, WE'LL LET YOU STAY.
THANK YOU.
HOW-EVER...
...I WILL DECIDE WHERE YOU ARE TO STAY.
WE DON'T WANT YOU WALKING AROUND ON YOUR OWN!
USE THE HOUSE IN FRONT OF THE CEMETERY, DOWN THE ROAD. GOT IT?
UNDER-STOOD.

HEY, HEY, OJII-CHAN!
LUNA WANTS TO SHOW THEM THE WAY!
HEY, IT'S OKAY, RIGHT?
わぁーい
......
AAAH! ME TOO!
I'LL GO TOO!!
NOW, NOW.
IT CAN'T BE HELPED. LUNA, YOU SHOW THEM THE WAY.
BE CAREFUL!
Heh heh heh!

NOW ...

......

LUNA'S HERE, SO YOU CAN RELAX!!

OH, SO YOU'RE LUNA-CHAN. NICE TO MEET YOU!
YUP. HAT'S OUR AME, NEE-HAN?

MY NAME'S PACIFICA.
PASEEKA?
PACIFICA.
PACILIKA?
......
W-WELL, LET'S JUST GO.
HMM ...

LUNA-CHAN, WHERE ARE THE OTHER PEOPLE FROM THIS VILLAGE?
OTHER PEOPLE?
YES, LIKE YOUR FATHER OR MOTHER.
UH-UH, I DON'T HAVE A DAD OR MOM!
JUST OJII-CHAN AND THE OTHER KIDS.
I WONDER WHERE THE OTHER PEOPLE HAVE GONE?
HMM...
UM...YOU KNOW, THEY SAY EVERYONE DIED A LOOOONG TIME AGO.
SO OJII-CHAN IS TAKING CARE OF US!
AH! THOSE ARE EVERYONE'S GRAVES.

ALL THE OTHER PEOPLE FROM THIS VILLAGE ARE BURIED HERE?
?!

I WONDER WHAT COULD HAVE HAPPENED?
DID YOU PUT THESE FLOWERS HERE, LUNA-CHAN?
OJII-CHAN DID.
HE SAID THOSE FLOWERS ARE RARE AND YOU CAN ONLY SEE THEM NEXT TO THIS VILLAGE.
THAT WOULD MAKE THE VILLAGERS BURIED HERE VERY HAPPY, HE SAID.
ALLY?
YEAH, I THINK SO TOO.
I'M SURE...

...THEY'RE PLEASED IN HEAVEN.

PACIFICA, WE NEED TO GO. WE'RE GETTING UP EARLY TOMORROW.

YEAH.

WE WERE ABLE TO GET AWAY FROM THOSE PURGERS, BUT I DON'T THINK THEY'LL GIVE UP SO EASILY.
WELL, THANK YOU! TAKE CARE!
SEE YOU LATER!

TONIGHT WE CAN SLEEP WITHOUT SEEING STARS!!
YEAH. WE NEED TO GET SOME REST.

?!

THAT'S --

HE DID AN EXCELLENT JOB OF GOING UNDETECTED.
YES.

HE'S AMAZING ISN'T HE?

WHO ON EARTH IS HE?

SHANNON-NII! THERE AREN'T ENOUGH BEDS, SO YOU'LL HAVE TO SLEEP ON THE FLOOR, OKAY?!
PFF!
GOOD GRIEF!
HEAVEN. THERE IS NO SUCH PLACE FOR YOU.
DEATH TO THE POISON!!!
POISON ...
... SCRAP-PED PRIN-CESS.
A BEING THAT SHOULD NOT HAVE BEEN BORN.

BECAUSE YOU EXIST, PEOPLE WILL BECOME UNHAPPY.
OW!
S-STOP IT!
WHY WERE YOU BORN? WHY ARE YOU ALIVE?!
YOU MUST DIE!
THIS HAPPENED BECAUSE OF YOU.

IF YOU HADN'T LIVED, THESE GRAVES WOULD NOT BE HERE.
NO!
EVERY PLACE YOU GO IS FILLED WITH CORPSES!!
STOP IT!!
ONEE-CHAN.

ONEE-CHAN!
UGH...
HMM?
EEEEEHHHH!
LET'S PLAY, NEE-CHAN.
ONEE-CHAN, IT'S ALL RED UNDER YOUR EYES.
AH, YEAH. I HAD A BAD DREAM.
Okay.
WHAT IND OF REAM?

A DREAM THAT MADE ME VERY UPSET.
YOU KNOW... I DON'T HAVE ANY PARENTS EITHER.
......
REALLY? YOU DON'T HAVE A MOM OR A DAD EITHER, PACIFICA-ONEECHAN?
NOPE.
SHANNON-NII AND RAQUEL-NEE ARE MY ONLY FAMILY.

IT SEEMS LIKE WHEN I'M AROUND, I CAUSE PROBLEMS FOR EVERYONE.
WITH ME AROUND, I MAKE EVERYONE UNHAPPY.
THE SCRAPPED PRINCESS--THE POISON THAT WILL DESTROY THE WORLD.
I MIGHT JUST BE WORTHLESS .
NOOOO!
ぶん
YOU CAN'T SAY THAT!
ぶん
LUNA, TOO. I ASKED OJII-CHAN AND THE OTHERS IF LUNA WAS WORTHLESS.
あた
OJII-CHAN GOT MAD AT ME.
HE SAID LUNA IS VERY PRECIOUS TO OJII-CHAN AND SHE SHOULDN'T SAY THOSE THINGS.

クス
AHA! HE SAYS THE SAME THING AS SHANNON-NII.
?
WHENEVER WE GO SOMEWHERE AND THINGS GET DANGEROUS OR HARD, SHANNON-NII SAYS...
YOU ARE PRECIOUS FAMILY.
WE'LL PROTECT YOU.
THAT' WHAT HE SAYS
PACIFICA-ONEECHAN IS THE SAME AS LUNA!
EVEN IF THINGS ARE HARD, LET'S DO OUR BEST TOGETHER! NO GIVING UP!
Yeah!

NO GIVING UP, HUH?
PACIFICA, YOU LOOK A LOT BETTER THAN YOU DID THIS MORNING.
YEAH. SOMEONE CHEERED ME UP.
BECAUSE THOSE KIDS ARE GOING THROUGH TOUGH TIMES AND HAVEN'T GIVEN UP...
...I WON'T GIVE UP EITHER.

HMMM.

ONII-CHAN, WHAT ARE YOU HANGING AROUND THERE FOR?

HMM?

OH, I THOUGHT I WOULD GO THANK JII-SAN FOR GIVING US A PLACE TO STAY.

JII-CHAN SHOULD BE THE CEMETE RIGHT NOW

THE CEMETERY?

HE PRAYS THERE EVERY MORNING.

TOMOR-ROW...

WHY DOES TOMORROW COME?
HUH?
FOR ME, TOMORROW NEVER COMES.
EVER SINCE THAT DAY...

I DON'T NEED A TOMORROW FOR MYSELF ANYMORE.

I HAVE DEVOTED EVERYTHING TO THE CHILDREN'S TOMORROW.

I WILL PROTECT THOSE CHILDREN EVEN IF I HAVE TO GIVE UP EVERYTHING ELSE.

WHAT HAPPENED BETWEEN YOU AND THOSE CHILDREN?!

JII-CHAAAN! I HAVE BAD NEWS.
LUNA WENT OUT BY HERSELF TO PICK FLOWERS.
WHAT ?!!
THAT P
IS STILL
DANGER
FOR H
THEN WE'LL GO BRING HER BACK.
SHANNON!
RAQUEL, GOOD TIMING. LOOK--
THEY'RE COMING THIS WAY.

?!
THEY? WHAT ARE YOU TALKING ABOUT?
PURGERS.
MAUSEL'S ...
...ASSASSIN CORPS?!

Chapter Eleven: Atonement Part Two

THE ONES CHASING AFTER US...
...ARE PURGERS.
OF ALL THINGS.
MAUSEL'S ASSASSIN CORPS.
I'M SORRY. WE DIDN'T MEAN TO GET YOU INVOLVED.
WE'LL HURRY AND LEAVE THE VILLAGE.
IN THE MEANTIME, JII-SAN, YOU GO GET LUNA.
IT'S SELESS.
LIKE YOU, THIS VILLAGE HAS BEEN FORSAKEN BY GOD.

THIS PLACE, THIS VILLAGE WAS DESTROYED BY MAUSEL IN THEIR HERETIC HUNT.
?!
IF THEY KNEW THERE WERE SURVIVORS...
...THEY WON'T LET THEM OFF SO EASY.
......

I'LL TAKE CARE OF IT.
MEANWHILE, YOU TAKE THE CHILDREN SOMEWHERE SAFE.
AND IN EXCHANGE ...
...I WOULD LIKE YOU TO HIDE PACIFICA UNTIL THE FIGHT IS OVER.
OH YEAH... BUT LUNA-CHAN.

PACIFICA?
I'LL GET LUNA-CHAN!!
?!
SIGH.

ポリ ポリ
LOOK, PACIFICA, YOU'RE THE ONE THEY'RE AFTER!
I KNOW THAT!
I HATE IT WHEN EVERYONE IS DOING SOMETHING AND I CAN'T DO ANYTHING!
HOW IS SHE SO STRONG?!
I DON'T WANT ANY REGRETS. THAT'S WHY!!
WE
DERSTAND.
L FIND OUT
ERE LUNA-
AN IS USING
MAGIC.

SHANNON-NII, RAQUEL-NEE, THANK YOU.
JII-SAN, TAKE THE CHILDREN AND FIND SHELTER.
I WISH I'D HAD SUCH STRENGTH...
I UNDER-STAND.
...BACK THEN.

HAA!
HAA!
MMM.
AHH!
LOOK OUT!!

YOU'RE SAFE.

HEY!

IT'S TOO DANGEROUS FOR YOU TO COME HERE BY YOURSELF!!

LOOK, YOU HURT YOUR LEG.

BUT

AH, WELL.

WE'LL TALK ABOUT IT LATER. RIGHT NOW, WE NEED TO GET BACK TO OJII-CHAN.

OJII-
CHAN.
LUNA.

LUNA, ARE
YOU HURT?!
ES. BUT
'S OKAY.
EE-CHAN
LPED ME.

SHE JUST
SCRAPED
HER LEG A
LITTLE.
I
SEE.
OLD YOU
MANY
IMES
TO GO
ERE BY
RSELF.

I'M SORRY.
BUT I REALLY...
...I REALLY WANTED TO GIVE ONEE-CHAN SOME FLOWERS.
I WANTED HER MOM AND DAD IN HEAVEN TO BE HAPPY.
REALLY? I SEE.
LUNA-CHAN.
THANK YOU.

OH! WHERE'S OJII-SAN?

THERE ARE FOUR OF THE ENEMY.

THE SPELL RAQUEL CAST ON ME WILL STRENGTHEN ME TEMPORARILY.

THIS SPELL CAN RAISE PEOPLE'S HIDD ABILITIES TEMPORARIL

BUT WHEN THE EFFECT WEARS OFF, AS MUCH AS IT DREW OUT WILL REBOUND BACK AT YOU.

IF I FOUGHT THEM FAIRLY, I WOULDN'T STAND A CHANCE.

AND IF THEY GET TOO CLOSE, I WON'T HAVE A CHANCE TO USE MAGIC.

SO IF I'M GOING TO USE IT, IT HAS TO BE NOW!!

...HERMOD!
MOUNT MY FLESH...

ONE...

TWO...
haa
haa
THREE...

ALL RIGHT. ONE LEFT.
THE REBOUND?!
DAMN! IS THAT ALL I CAN DO?

?!

TOO MANY PEOPLE...

...HAVE DIED IN THIS VILLAGE!!

NO!
JII-SAN!!

WHY... WHY?!
IT WASN'T FOR YOU.
HAA...
EHH...
IT DOESN'T MATTER TO ME WHO YOU PEOPLE ARE.
DON'T TALK. I'LL TREAT YOUR WOUNDS.
UH! IT'S NO GOOD. HE GOT HIS VITALS.
SO DON'T WORRY ABOUT ME.

I WAS
HERET
EXAMIN

IT CAN'T BE...

I HAD ORDERS FROM THE CHURCH TO DESTROY VILLAGES OF HERETICS.

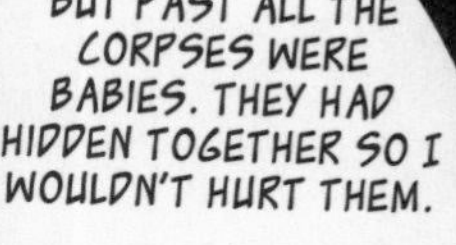

IT WAS THEN THAT I REALIZED FOR THE FIRST TIME...

.THAT I AD DONE METHING THAT I ULD NOT UNDO.

IS THAT WHY YOU WERE SAYING THAT YOUR TOMORROW WAS FOR THE CHILDREN?

AFTER MEETING YOUR SISTER, IT MADE ME WONDER. I JUST DON'T KNOW ANYMORE.

MY INTENTION WAS TO ACCEPT FATE, BUT I WAS JUST BEING CARRIED ALONG BY FATE.

YOUR SISTER ...

...WENT TO LOOK FOR LUNA, EVEN THOUGH HER OWN LIFE WAS IN DANGER.

WHAT MAKES YOUR DESTINY, YOUR FUTURE...
...IS YOUR OWN WILL.
SO I WANTED TO END THE CONFLICT WITH MY PAST...
...BY COMPARING THE PURGERS TO MY OLD SELF.
I'M SORRY.
PLEASE DO NOT WORRY ABOUT ME.
YOU WILL CONTINUE TO PROTECT THE GIRL, RIGHT?

THEN LIVE, AND PROTECT HER TO THE VERY END!!
ITHOUT BEING ARRIED ALONG Y FATE, WITH YOUR OWN POWER...
...THE FUTURE IS YOURS.

WILL YOU REAL BE AL RIGHT
ALL OF YOU, TAKE CARE!!
YUP. BECAUSE THIS IS OUR HOME.
PACIFICA-NEECHAN!
PLEASE COME TO PLAY WITH US AGAIN, OKAY?!
I DON'T KNOW WHEN IT'LL BE...
...BUT I WILL DEFINITELY COME TO SEE YOU, LUNA-CHAN.

EVERYONE...
I THINK I WILL...
LUTEA?
I THINK I ILL STAY HERE.
I WANT TO HELP THESE CHILDREN. WILL YOU ALLOW ME TO?

YOU DECIDED ON YOUR OWN, LUTEA.
WE WILL RESPECT YOUR DECISION.
......
TAKE CARE LUTEA
THANK YOU FOR EVERYTHING.
THANK YOU. YOU TAKE CARE TOO.

HEY, SHANNON-NII!
WAS IT OKAY TO PUT OJII-SAN'S GRAVE THERE?
H. I THINK AT'S THE T PLACE.
IF HE'S THERE, HE CAN WATCH OVER THE CHILDREN!!

EPILOGUE

Ojii-chan, it's been ten years since...

OH! WHERE IS LUNA-SAN?

I DUNNO. ISN'T SHE WITH JII-SAN AGAIN?

THEN I WILL GO GET HER.

Everyone is happy and healthy in the village that you, Pacifica-san and the others protected.
Little by little, this village is becoming livelier.

Everyone else is getting married and having children.

There's even a wonderful staircase in the place you told me was dangerous to go to by myself.

What hasn't changed is the view of the village from here.

LUNA-SAN.

IT'S ALMOST TIME.

AH! SORRY.

YOUR GROOM IS WAITING.

WHAT WERE YOU TALKING ABOUT WITH OJII-SAN?

OH...
I WAS TELLING HIM ABOUT MY WEDDING AND...

...ASKING HIM TO ALWAYS WATCH OVER ME.
MY!

SAY, LUTEA...
YES?
I WONDER HOW PACIFICA-ONEECHAN AND THE OTHERS ARE DOING?
I'M SURE THOSE THREE...
...ARE DOING JUST FINE.
To be continued in volume Three

SCRAPPED PRINCESS

Next Time In

The four priests who predicted the "Revelation of Grendel" are found dead, and Tasa, one of the priest's daughters, now seeks revenge on Pacifica. In the midst of a punitive team attack on the siblings, Tasa and Raging Bull, a hired assassin, come to their aid because Tasa wants to kill Pacifica herself. Tasa and Pacifica end up getting captured. If they are rescued in time, will Tasa still want the blood of the "Destruction Princess?"

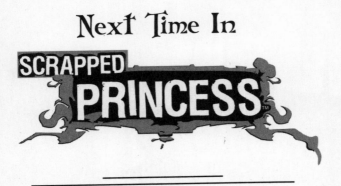

WWW.TOKYOPOP.COM/ROADSONG

STOP!

This is the back of the book.
You wouldn't want to spoil a great ending!

This book is printed "manga-style," in the authentic Japanese right-to-left format. Since none of the artwork has been flipped or altered, readers get to experience the story just as the creator intended. You've been asking for it, so TOKYOPOP® delivered: authentic, hot-off-the-press, and far more fun!

DIRECTIONS

If this is your first time reading manga-style, here's a quick guide to help you understand how it works.

It's easy... just start in the top right panel and follow the numbers. Have fun, and look for more 100% authentic manga from TOKYOPOP®!